Read to Me

Bible Stories for Preschoolers

Wonderful Things

Written by Daphna Flegal
Illustrated by Robert S. Jones

Note to Parents:

Enjoy sharing this storybook with your child. Each page has two parts: one for your child and one for you. The children's story is written in larger print. The adult text is written in smaller print on the left-hand page. The adult text will offer suggestions, explanations, and helpful ways you can use this storybook to share your faith with your young child.

Take time to read the adult text before reading the story to your child. This will help you be familiar with the ideas and explanations that correspond with the story line. It will also keep you from being distracted by the adult text when you share the story with your child.

As children grow in body, they also grow in faith. You will have many opportunities to help your child deepen his or her relationship with God. We hope that sharing this storybook with your child is one of those opportunities. Hold your child close beside you as you read. Let him or her feel the warmth of your touch and love as you tell the wonderful things God has done.

Wonderful things,
Wonderful things,
Tell of God's many wonderful things!

God's world is filled with many wonderful things! Young children delight in things that adults often take for granted. Take time to wonder with your child. Walk in the rain and splash in the puddles. Admire a ladybug. Count the stars in the night sky. And while you and your child are enjoying the many wonderful things that God has done, remember to thank God for rain, for ladybugs, and for stars.

4

Tell about sunshine,

Tell about rain,

Tell about . . .

Rainbows are wonderful things! Each time you see a rainbow, remind your child that the rainbow is a sign of God's promise to care for the earth. Help your child understand that God plans for each one of us to help take care of the earth. Involve your child in activities that help care for the earth, such as planting flowers, feeding the birds, and recycling. Remind your child that each of us has work to do in God's world.

rainbows!

Wonderful things,
Wonderful things,
Tell of God's many wonderful things!

Seeds are wonderful things! Examine many different kinds of seeds with your child. Blow dandelion seeds. Watch maple tree seeds twirl to the ground. Cut an apple in half to find a seed pattern in the shape of a star. Eat sunflower seeds. Roast pumpkin seeds. Remind your child about what grows from each kind of seed. Be sure to thank God for seeds!

Tell about planting,

8

Tell about corn,

Tell about . . .

9

Foods that grow from plants and trees are wonderful things! Many children are removed from direct experiences with how things grow in God's world. We get oranges from the grocery store, not from a tree. Help your child develop a better understanding of God's world by providing opportunities for your child to touch, taste, hear, smell, and see God's creation. Plant seeds and care for them. Squeeze your own orange juice, or pick your own strawberries. Say a thank-you prayer for food that grows on plants and trees.

Popcorn!

Wonderful things,
Wonderful things,
Tell of God's many wonderful things!

11

Our bodies are wonderful things! God plans for us to use our bodies and our minds as we grow and learn new things. Each time your child learns a new skill or outgrows a pair of shoes, remind your child that God plans for us to grow. Say a prayer, thanking God for your child's growth.

Tell about fingers,

Tell about toes,

Tell about . . .

Your child is a wonderful thing! Affirm your child as someone special. Listen to your child. Accept your child's thoughts and feelings. Remind your child that she or he is loved. Model God's love through your actions and words. Constantly "catch" your child doing things right.

Wonderful things,
Wonderful things,
Tell of God's many wonderful things!

I will praise you, LORD ... I will tell of all the wonderful things you have done.

Psalm 9:1, *Good News Bible*

Noah's Very Big Boat

Written by Susan Isbell
Illustrated by Robert S. Jones

18

God loved Noah, and Noah trusted God. Help
your child know that we can trust God to take care
of us just as Noah did. Your child will not be able
to picture how large the ark actually was. Help
your child know that the ark built by Noah
housed many animals and people and that it was
larger than your house.

20

Zzz, zzz, zzz! Noah cut the wood.
Wham, wham, wham! Noah hammered the wood.
Zzz, zzz, zzz! *Wham, wham, wham!*
Noah was building a boat.

A very **b-i-g** boat.

Imagine living several months inside a boat with lots of animals! Talk with your child and imagine together what the inside of the ark looked like. What would Noah need to keep the animals alive and safe for all those days? How would the animals sound?

22

Roar-r-r, roar-r-r. Qua-a-ck, qua-a-ck. N-e-i-gh, n-e-i-gh. Ribbit, ribbit. The animals came two by two. The animals went into the boat with Noah and his family.

The very **b-i-g** boat.

Rain and thunderstorms can be both frightening and beautiful. We have no reason to believe that Noah was frightened by the magnitude of the biblical storm. Talk about storms today and the rain in the story. Assure your child that although storms are scary, it will never rain enough to cover everything as it did in the time of Noah.

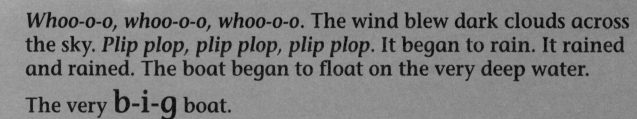

Whoo-o-o, whoo-o-o, whoo-o-o. The wind blew dark clouds across the sky. *Plip plop, plip plop, plip plop.* It began to rain. It rained and rained. The boat began to float on the very deep water.

The very b-i-g boat.

25

After several long months in the ark we can imagine the anticipation of Noah to set foot on dry land again. Help your child recall a time when rain or bad weather kept you inside. Did you plan what you would do when you could get out again? How did it feel to be out of the house after weather kept you in for a long time?

Rock, rock. Rock, rock. The boat rocked back and forth on the water for a very long time. *Plip plop plip.* Then the rain stopped. The boat rested on a very tall mountain.

The very b-i-g boat.

God had brought Noah and his family safely through the flood. We can imagine their joy at finally being able to leave the very big boat. Noah's family had protected the animals from harm in the ark. Just as Noah's family had trusted God, God had trusted Noah's family to protect and care for the animals inside the ark. What can your family do today to care for and help protect animals and God's creation?

Roar-r-r, roar-r-r. Qua-a-ck, qua-a-ck.
N-e-i-gh, n-e-i-gh. Ribbit, ribbit.
All the animals left the boat.
Noah and his family left the boat.

The very **b-i-g** boat.

29

Rainbows are one of the most cherished sights to be found in nature. As much as we enjoy spotting rainbows in the sky, like Noah, we cannot see a rainbow unless we experience the rain first. Help your child think of times and places that rainbows might be seen. Remind your child that a rainbow reminds us of God's promise to love and care for us, just as God cared for Noah.

O-o-h, o-o-h, o-o-h. A bow of colors appeared in the sky. It was a rainbow. Noah thanked God for keeping the animals and his family safe on the boat.

The very b-i-g boat.

Whenever a rainbow appears, I will remember my promise to you.

Genesis 9:14-15
Good News Bible
Adapted

Baby Moses

Written by Elizabeth Crocker
Illustrated by Nancy Munger

The arrival of a new baby is an event that is met with many mixed feelings. Like Miriam, young children are often elated with the new arrival, only to be confounded by the practical realities of a growing family. Talk with your child about happy feelings. Make a point of the fact that Bible people had many of the same feelings that people today have.

"A new baby brother!" said sister Miriam.
Miriam watched as Mother held the new baby in her arms.

Moses was born into a world that was not safe for him, but through the love and care of his mother, Miriam, and the princess, he survived. Do not dwell on the negative portions of this story, such as Pharaoh's order to kill Hebrew babies. Instead, emphasize that Miriam and Mother loved Moses, so they made a basket for him to keep him safe. Talk with your child about ways of showing love and care in your family.

"Oh, no!" said Miriam. "What about Pharaoh? He will not be happy about our new baby."

Moses' mother and sister made his basket waterproof by rubbing the inside with tar. Talk with your child about preparations you made for his or her arrival and the people who celebrated with you. If possible, show your child some baby things: clothes, a bathtub, or a bassinet. Find a baby doll and a basket. Invite your child to act out the story.

Pat, pat, pat went the sound of Mother's hands. Mother made a basket for the new baby.

41

Enjoy water play with your child. Let him or her experiment with things that float. Explain that the river was important to the Bible people. They depended on it for water to grow their food, to wash, and to drink. Talk about the ways that water is important to us today. By placing the baby in the reeds along the shore, Mother and Miriam ensured that the baby would be found and cared for.

Spla-a-ash, spla-a-ash went the water.
Mother and Miriam placed the basket gently in the river.

Help your child find Miriam in this picture. Tell him or her that Miriam waited and watched to see who would find the baby. Explain that the princess was Pharaoh's daughter. She lived in a beautiful palace. There Moses would be safe and happy. Emphasize that the princess, like Mother and Miriam, loved Moses.

"Look!" said the princess. "I found a baby!"
The princess took the baby from the basket.

The name Moses means "drawn out" or "born of." It was chosen for Moses because it described how the princess found him. In ancient Egypt children rescued from the Nile were considered special. Talk with your child about his or her name and how it was chosen. Talk with your child about ways that he or she is special to you. Emphasize that in Bible times and today, all people are special to God.

"Moses!" said the princess. "I will name you Moses!" The princess cuddled Moses as she held him tenderly in her arms.

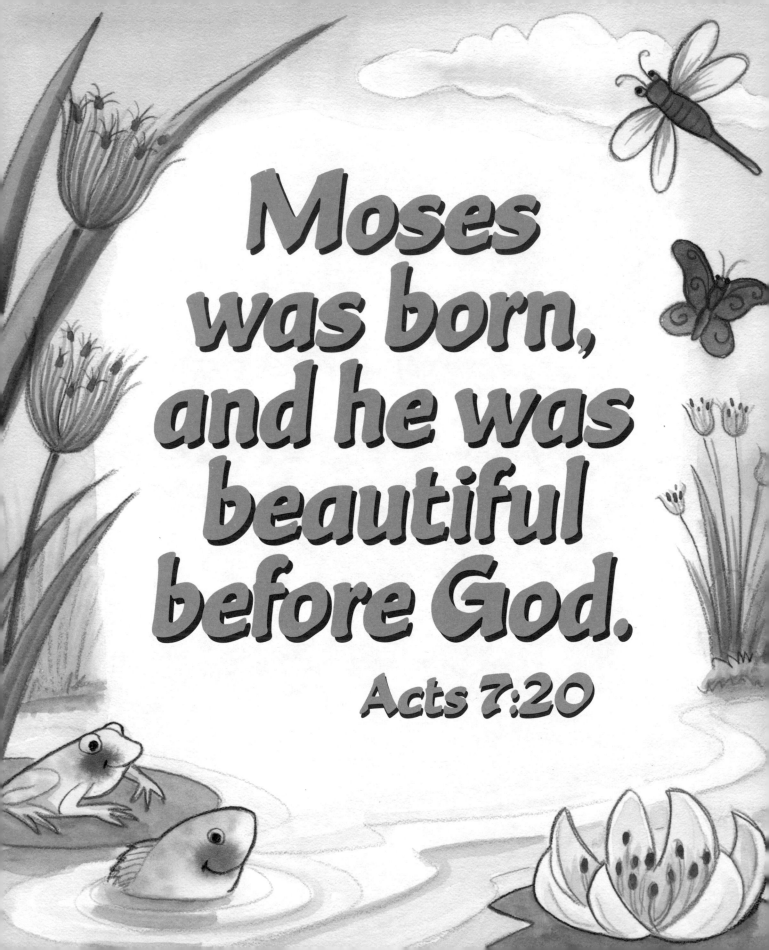

Moses was born, and he was beautiful before God.

Acts 7:20

David Counts His Sheep

Written by Daphna Flegal
Illustrated by Nancy Munger

Young children have trouble understanding the concept of long ago. They may not know what a shepherd does or is unless you explain. Help your child understand that a shepherd is someone who takes care of sheep, much as you take care of your child. Talk about some of the things you do to take care of your child, like making sure he or she has food to eat, has clothes to wear, and gets enough sleep.

"1, 2, 3," counted David. David is a shepherd. He takes care of the sheep.

Many young children have not actually seen a sheep. Use the pictures in this storybook to show the children illustrations of a shepherd and sheep. If possible, take your child to a petting zoo or farm that has sheep that your child may see and touch.

54

1, 2, 3. Can you find three of David's sheep?

It was David's responsibility to take care of the family's sheep. David's duties as a shepherd included leading the sheep to food and water and making sure that the flock was kept safe. You may find it helpful to relate the job of a shepherd to how we care for pets. We must feed our pets and make sure our pets are kept safe.

"1, 2, 3, 4," counted David. David led the sheep up the hillside. The sheep ate the soft, green grass. The sheep drank the cool water of the stream.

Encourage your child to pretend to be David. Let him or her use stuffed animals to be the sheep. Or let your child pretend to be the sheep and you be the shepherd. Pretend to lead your child to get a drink of water from a stream. *Baa* like a sheep. Enjoy playing with your child.

58

1, 2, 3, 4. Can you find four of David's sheep?

Talk about a shepherd camping out at night and staying with the sheep to protect the sheep. In Bible times a shepherd would gather the sheep into a sheepfold or cave. The shepherd would stay at the opening to make sure no wild animals or robbers could get to the sheep.

"1, 2, 3, 4, 5," counted David. David led the sheep to the cave. The sheep knew that David would keep them safe for the night.

A good shepherd loved his sheep. The sheep knew the shepherd's voice and trusted the shepherd. The story of David reminds us that God is like a good shepherd. God loves us and cares for us. We can trust God. Find a quiet place to sit with your child. Read your child Psalm 23 from your family Bible. Say a prayer thanking God for God's love and care.

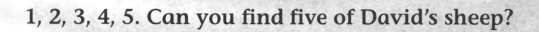
1, 2, 3, 4, 5. Can you find five of David's sheep?

The
Lord
is my
shepherd.

Psalm 23:1

Jesus Is Born

Notes to Parents by Carol Krau
Story by Daphna Flegal
Illustrated by Marvin Jarboe

You can help your child experience this much-loved story through concrete images of sight, sound, smell, and touch. When you read each page, stop to talk about what is happening in the story. Ask your child to imagine riding a donkey or to show you how he or she would walk if tired. Point to Mary and Joseph on each page to reinforce who they are.

Clippity clop! Clippity Clop! Mary rode the donkey to Bethlehem. Joseph walked beside her. Mary and Joseph were tired. It was a long trip.

Clippity clop! Clippity clop! Joseph led Mary and the donkey to the inn at Bethlehem.

Your child may not be familiar with the word *inn*. To explain where Joseph looked for a room, talk about motels or hotels. If your family has ever spent the night at a hotel, your child may remember how tired her or she felt after a long day's drive. Ask your child: "How do you think Mary and Joseph felt when they finally arrived at the inn after their long trip?"

Knock! Knock! Joseph knocked on the door of the inn. "May we have a room for the night?" Joseph asked the innkeeper. "My wife is going to have a baby, and we need to rest."

71

Many children will not know what a stable is. It will be hard for them to imagine Mary and Joseph's relief when the innkeeper told them they could sleep in the stable. Who would want to sleep in a barn? Remind your child that Joseph and Mary were very tired. Since Mary was going to have a baby, she needed rest.

"I'm sorry," said the innkeeper. "All our rooms are full."

Sadly, Mary and Joseph turned to walk away.

"Wait!" called the innkeeper to Joseph. "You may sleep in the stable. You will be warm with the animals. You may sleep on the hay."

Young children will enjoy making animal noises. Doing so will help them understand what it was like for Mary and Joseph to stay in the stable. Let your child pretend to be a lamb or a calf. Direct your child to "baa" or "moo" loudly, then more quietly, until he or she finally "falls asleep."

B-a-a! B-a-a! M-o-o! M-o-o!
Mary and Joseph heard the animals
making noises in the stable. Mary and
Joseph were glad to have a warm place
to rest. Soon even the animals were quiet.
Everyone was asleep.

Talk about how excited Mary and Joseph were when Jesus was born. Tell your child about his or her birth. Look at pictures of your child as a newborn. Let your child know that you waited eagerly for her or his birth, just as Mary and Joseph waited for Jesus to be born. If your child is adopted, talk about how both you and his or her birth mother waited.

Then a wonderful thing happened!
During the night, Mary's baby was born.
Mary and Joseph named the baby Jesus.

Mary wrapped baby Jesus in soft cloths
to keep him warm. She sang softly as she
rocked baby Jesus to sleep.

Tell your child that God planned for Jesus to be born so that we might know God's love. One way we can see God's love is through the love of our families.

Say a prayer with your child, thanking God for families, for love, and for Jesus.

Joseph smiled at Mary and the baby.
Mary and Joseph were happy that baby Jesus
was born.

(Based on Luke 2:1-7.)

You will name him Jesus.

Luke 1:31

Just Like Me and You!

Written by Daphna Flegal
Illustrated by Nell Fisher

Young children often have difficulty understanding that the baby born at Christmas is the same person as the man we call Jesus. You can help your child begin to understand the connection by talking about how Jesus grew.

Jesus learned things as he

grew.

85

Just like me, and

Help your child identify with the growing Jesus. Talk about the many ways your child is growing. Jesus grew in those same ways. Your child grew from a baby to a boy or girl. Jesus grew from a baby to a boy. Jesus was three (and four and five) years old, just as your child is three (or four or five).

Use this story as an opportunity to compliment your child on all the things he or she can do now that he or she could not do as a baby. Encourage your child to show you something she or he can do now that she or he could not do as a baby.

He learned to walk and run and jump.
He learned to stand up tall.

89

He learned to talk and laugh and sing. He learned

As a young boy, Jesus would have learned about God from his family. Boys in Hebrew homes were taught at home by their mothers until they were five or six years old, when they attended synagogue school. Girls were taught by their mothers until they were married. Fathers taught their sons a trade, so Joseph probably taught Jesus the skill of carpentry.

God loves us all.

91

Constantly remind your child that God loves her or him. God loved your child when he or she was a baby, and God loves your child now. And while you're at it, remind your child that you love him or her as well.

God loved Jesus

as he grew.

93

Children in Bible times learned about the laws of God from their parents, who handed down the stories of faith within the family. Parents encouraged their children to ask questions about the faith. Encourage your child to ask questions about the faith. Help your child learn about God as she or he grows—just as Jesus learned about God as he grew.

Just like me, and

just like you!

Jesus and the Children

Written by Daphna Flegal
Illustrated by Nell Fisher

98

This story shows Jesus' great love for children. So great was this love that Jesus said everyone should be more like the children in God's world. All children need to feel loved and wanted.

"Come!" said Mother. "Come and see Jesus."
Mother and daughter came.

Help your child understand that Jesus was
a very special person. Crowds followed him
everywhere. Many people wanted to hear
him speak. Many others wanted to touch him
and be healed.

"Come!" said Father. "Come and see Jesus."
Father and son came.

It must have been very hard for the parents and their children to push through the crowds and get close enough to see Jesus. Your child will be able to identify with being small and not always being able to see and hear what is happening around him or her.

"Come!" said Sister.
"Come and see Jesus."
Sister and brother came.

Remind your child that Jesus' friends were not intentionally being mean. Their actions had nothing to do with whether or not they liked children. They were just trying to take care of Jesus. They probably thought Jesus was too busy to talk with children. Ask your child, "How do you think the children felt when they were told to go home?"

"Stop!" said the man. "You cannot see Jesus."
The children stopped. They turned to go away.

Help your child understand that Jesus spent time with the children because he wanted to, not to satisfy their parents or to teach his friends a lesson. Jesus spent time with children because he genuinely loved being with them. If your child has special adult friends, help him or her understand why those friends are so special. Adult friends of children often possess the same patience, gentleness, and ability to listen that made Jesus special.

"Come!" said Jesus.
"Let the children come to me."

109

Remind your child that Jesus not only loved children in Bible times, but also that Jesus still loves children today. Sing "Jesus Loves Me" with your child. Remind your child that this story comes from the Bible.

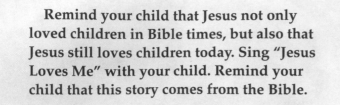

110

And the children came.

111

Let the little children come to me.

Mark 10:14

A Very Happy Day

Written by Joyce Riffe
Illustrated by Nell Fisher

115

Palm Sunday is a happy time and a time
of celebration in the church. This is the day
we remember that the people joyfully
welcomed Jesus as he rode a donkey into
Jerusalem. Help your child feel the happy
anticipation conveyed by the words and
rhythm of this story as you read it together.
Something exciting is happening!

116

Hurry! Hurry!
Mothers and fathers hurried into the city.
Boys and girls skipped along beside them.
Jesus was coming!

Children sense the emotions of others. They are usually aware of family crisis times and, in the same way, easily become caught up in happy, exciting family times. Children in the crowd that welcomed Jesus must have caught the feelings of that special moment from their parents and others. You can help your child feel a special excitement about Jesus too.

Listen! Listen!

Fathers and mothers told their friends the good news. Girls and boys knew something special was about to happen. Jesus was coming!

When Jesus entered Jerusalem, people waved palm branches and spread them on the road to welcome Jesus. We often celebrate happy times and special occasions with flowers or plants. Gather or buy some simple greenery for your child's room to mark this special day.

Quick! Quick!

Mothers and fathers spread their coats on the road.
Boys and girls waved green palm branches.
Jesus was coming!

121

Jesus rode into Jerusalem on a donkey. Has your child ever seen a donkey or a horse or anyone riding such an animal? Help your child think of differences in Bible times and today. Ask your child why Jesus did not ride in a car. Help your child know that in Jesus' time, people walked or rode animals or traveled by boat.

122

Clop! Clop!

Fathers and mothers heard the donkey coming closer and closer. Girls and boys ran to meet Jesus and the donkey. Jesus was coming!

The people who welcomed Jesus to Jerusalem knew that Jesus was special. They had heard about his teaching and healing. They knew that he spoke authoritatively about God and God's ways. Help your child also recognize that Jesus is special. Recall with your child the familiar stories about Jesus that are in the Bible—Jesus being born, Jesus visiting with the children, and Jesus helping others. Tell your child that Jesus is special because he shows us how God loves us and wants us to live.

Look! Look!

Mothers and fathers saw Jesus riding on the donkey.
Boys and girls saw Jesus smile at them as he rode by.
Jesus was here!

The people's cry of "Hosanna!" was a shout of welcome and joy. Help your child know that we can praise God too. Encourage your child to think of many good gifts that we have from God—food, family members, beautiful things in God's natural world, and the church. We are thankful and can praise God for Jesus too. Say a simple, spontaneous prayer of thanks and praise with your child for God's gifts and, especially, for Jesus.

Hosanna! Hosanna!

Fathers and mothers shouted welcome to Jesus.
Girls and boys sang loud, happy songs.
It was a very happy day.

127

Hosanna!
Mark 11:9

A Special Meal with Friends

Written by Susan Isbell
Illustrated by Lyn Martin

131

Children enjoy having friends over and sharing special meals together. Times around a dinner table are times when special thoughts can be shared and special memories made.

The meal that Jesus shared with his disciples was the biblical beginning of our sacrament of Holy Communion. Help your child understand the Bible story about Jesus' special supper with his friends in terms of the meal, the love of friends, and the memories that were made, instead of in the abstract terms of the symbolism of the body and blood of Christ.

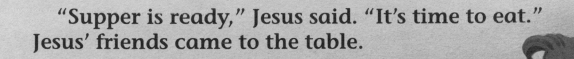

"Supper is ready," Jesus said. "It's time to eat."
Jesus' friends came to the table.

133

Children need to know that the food Jesus shared with his friends was real and normal food. The Passover meal was an annual observance when the Jewish people recalled their hasty preparation for the flight from Egypt as told in the Book of Exodus. Traditional Passover foods include roasted lamb shank, bitter herbs, and unleavened bread. These were not unusual foods for people of Bible times.

"Thank you, God, for this food," Jesus said.
His friends were ready to eat.

As they came to the meal, Jesus' disciples may not have realized that this meal was any different from other Passover celebrations. They came ready to eat and to be with one another as they observed one of their religious traditions. Jesus' words as he broke the bread, "Eat this in memory of me," no doubt took on new meaning after the events of the following several days.

What is important for children is that Jesus wanted his friends to remember his great love for them each time they ate together.

"The food is good," said Jesus. "Eat it and remember that I love you." His friends were hungry. They ate the bread and meat that Jesus gave them.

Children think in concrete terms. Hearing a minister read the words from Scripture about eating the body and drinking the blood can be extremely frightening to young children. Children begin thinking abstractly at a much later age. Until they can begin to understand symbolism, children will best understand this story as a way Jesus reminded his friends of his love for them.

138

"The drink is cold," said Jesus.
"Drink it and remember that I love you."
Jesus' friends were thirsty. They drank all
that was in the cup.

Jesus tried his best to prepare his disciples for the time when he would no longer live among them. His instructions to eat and drink "in memory of me" were one way of doing just that.

Friendships are important to all of us, especially to children. If your family has moved, or if your children have friends who have moved or friends who live in other places, your child will be better able to understand how we remember people and their love for us even when they are not present with us.

"You are my best friends," Jesus said.
"Each time you eat together, remember that I am your
friend." His friends told Jesus that they would remember.

Children know that their parents love them even when their parents are not with them. Love is experienced in many ways, not only between parent and child, but also between good friends. Just as children might relate to friends in other places, they also might recall grandparents or other relatives who are seen infrequently but are loved just the same. Help your child know that love is not dependent on the loved one being present.

The love that Jesus had for his friends was not one-sided. The disciples had come to love and depend on Jesus. It was for him that they gave up their normal lives. Their time with him changed their lives and the rest of the world forever.

Help your child know that Jesus' friends did remember Jesus each time they shared a special meal together, even when Jesus was not with them. We do the same today as we remember Jesus' love for us each time our church family and friends have Communion.

142

"You are my best friends," Jesus said. "Each time you eat together, remember that I love you." His friends told Jesus that they would remember.

(Based on Luke 22:7-20.)

Lydia Becomes a Follower of Jesus

Written by Daphna Flegal
Illustrated by Nell Fisher

Lydia was probably a wealthy and important woman in her community. Purple cloth was expensive. The pigment needed to dye fabric purple came from mollusks. Each shell yielded only a small amount of dye, so only the wealthy could afford to own purple fabric. In fact, the phrase "the purple" referred not only to the color of the cloth, but also to the cloth itself, the people who wore it, and to the classes who could afford it. Encourage your child to find the things that are colored purple in this storybook. Let your child experiment with the color purple. Have your child color with purple crayons or paint with purple paint. Squeeze red and blue food coloring into water and let your child stir the colors together to make purple.

148

Lydia was a woman who lived long, long ago.
She lived in a busy city. She sold purple cloth.

Can you find Lydia? She's dressed in purple.

Prayer must have been important to Lydia. Remind your child that prayer is also important to us. Explain to your child that prayer is talking to God. We can talk to God anytime and anyplace. We know that God will always hear us when we pray. Say a prayer right now, thanking God for time to sit and tell a story to your child.

Lydia loved God. She liked to meet with other women who loved God. Lydia and the women sat beside the river and prayed together.

Can you find Lydia? Can you find the flower?

Paul went on long trips to tell people about Jesus. It was on one of his trips that Paul met Lydia. Explain to your child that there were no cars or airplanes in Bible times. Paul and his friends walked, traveled by ship, or possibly rode donkeys or horses from place to place. Let your child pretend to travel like Paul. Show your child a pair of sandals. Explain that people in Bible times often walked along dusty roads. Let your child float boats in the bathtub or in a dishpan. Explain that Paul sometimes traveled by boat.

Paul was a follower of Jesus. He saw Lydia and her friends sitting beside the river. Paul told Lydia and her friends all about Jesus. Lydia listened. She became a follower of Jesus.

Can you find Lydia? Can you find the flower and the basket of purple cloth?

Lydia and her whole household were baptized. This was a sign that in her home, Christian beliefs would be practiced. What are some signs in your home that show you are Christian? Are there Bibles in your home? Do you pray before meals? Before bedtime? Do you display your child's Sunday school projects on your refrigerator? Talk with your child about some of the things that your family does that show you are followers of Jesus.

154

Lydia told her family about Jesus. They all became followers of Jesus. Paul baptized Lydia and her family in the river.

Can you find Lydia? Can you find the flower, the basket of purple cloth, and the fish?

155

Many people learned about Jesus because Lydia became a Christian. Tell your child about someone who helped you learn about Jesus. Then talk about the people who are helping your child learn about Jesus. Say a prayer with your child, thanking God for all the people you named.

Lydia invited Paul and his friends to stay at her house.
They told many people about Jesus.

*Can you find Lydia? Can you find the flower, the basket of
purple cloth, the fish, and the purple grapes?*

You can help your child love God more and more. Go with your child to Sunday school and church. Read your child Bible stories. Pray with your child. Look for things that can remind you and your child about God in the course of your everyday life. Notice a beautiful sunset, and say a prayer thanking God for the pink and purple clouds. Celebrate your child's physical growth and remind your child that God plans for our bodies to grow. When your child is coloring with purple crayons, say something like, "I'm glad God planned for so many colors in the world."

158

Lydia and her family were followers of Jesus. Their love for God kept growing more and more.

Can you find Lydia? Can you find the flower, the basket of purple cloth, the fish, the purple grapes, and the purple cloud?

159